stickyfaith
service guide

student journal

stickyfaith
service guide

student journal

how serving others
changes you

Kara Powell
& Brad M. Griffin

ZONDERVAN

Sticky Faith Service Guide, Student Journal
Copyright © 2009, 2016 by Kara E. Powell and Brad M. Griffin

Previously published as *Deep Justice Journeys Student Journal.*

This title is also available as a Zondervan ebook. Visit www.zondervan.com/ebooks.

Requests for information should be addressed to:
Zondervan, 3900 *Sparks Dr. SE, Grand Rapids, Michigan* 49546

ISBN 978-0-310-52423-6

Cover design: *Brand Navigation*
Cover photography: © *Pixelrobot / Dreamstime.com*
Interior imagery: © *Frank Fiedler / Shutterstock®,* © *PhotoDisc,*
    © *Evgeny Atamanenko / Shutterstock®*
Interior design: *Kait Lamphere*

Printed in the United States of America

HB 06.01.2017

CONTENTS

PART 1: BEFORE: FRAMING

PART 2: DURING:
EXPERIENCE AND REFLECTION

PART 3: AFTER: DEBRIEF

PART 4: AFTER:
ONGOING TRANSFORMATION

INITIAL STEPS

GETTING THE MOST OUT OF YOUR SERVICE TRIP OR LOCAL PROJECT

THAT GREAT "SERVICE HIGH."

If you've been involved in service work before, you probably know the feeling. After four days in Mexico or four hours of feeding the homeless in your city, you're ready to change the world.

But then you walk back into life as usual ...

Your mom asks you to empty the dishwasher.

Your friends at school make fun of you when you invite the new kid to grab coffee after school.

And your cousin wants you to go drinking with him.

Short-term mission trips and other service opportunities can help you take three steps forward in your walk of faith. But then you get back home and it seems like you get yanked 2.93 steps backward.

Sure, you're making progress. But if you do the math, it's only .07 total steps forward. Not nearly as much as you'd hoped.

What if we told you it didn't have to be that way?

What if we told you that although we can't guarantee you won't slip backward at all, we can help you and your youth ministry figure out how to experience real, lasting change? We call that change that *sticks*.

This book is intended to help you and thousands of other teenagers figure out how to experience all God has to offer you before, during, and after your service projects. We've talked with some other great teenagers, parents, youth workers, and researchers about how you can make the most of your service. Here's the model we hope you and your team follow:

The Sticky Faith Service Model[1]

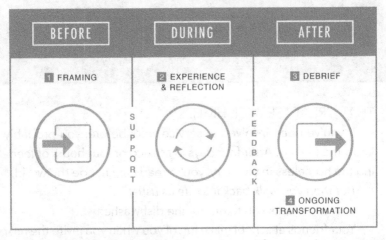

Let's unpack what all those arrows mean for your own journey and for the journal you hold in your hands.

STEP 1. BEFORE: FRAMING

A successful service or mission experience starts when you frame the sometimes mind-blowing and other times menial experiences that await you. Getting ready for a mission trip involves much more than just raising money, learning a drama, or deciding what to pack. This journal helps you prepare emotionally, mentally, spiritually, and relationally for what lies ahead.

STEP 2. DURING:
EXPERIENCE AND REFLECTION

During your work, you and your friends will be placed in situations and activities that will stretch you. Maybe you'll use new skill muscles in a cross-cultural setting that's unfamiliar to you. Or your group will get tired, cranky, and hungry—and the glue that has united you up to that point will start to dissolve. This journal gives space for you to stop and catch your breath from time to time (every few hours or maybe every day or so) and probe the deeper meaning behind all you're thinking and feeling.

STEP 3. AFTER:
DEBRIEF

At the end of your trip, as your mind and your group's minivans are starting to head home, you're now ready to debrief your experience. Maybe it's the last day of your short-term mission trip as you take a bit of time to relax and have fun. Or perhaps it's when you hit a coffee shop with your group right after you've visited patients at the local children's hospital. Either way, the goal is for you to take time right after the "work" is completed to start thinking about the even harder work of long-term change.

STEP 4. AFTER:
ONGOING TRANSFORMATION

The final step of ongoing transformation helps you move beyond that "service high" to living out justice in the midst of the ups and downs of everyday life. This journal helps you connect the dots between having lunch with a homeless man in Detroit and having lunch with a new kid in your school cafeteria one month later.

THROUGH IT ALL:
SUPPORT AND FEEDBACK

We hope you're walking through this journey with a team of friends and adults. But in addition to your team, you can also seek support and feedback from your congregation and the denominational group or short-term missions agency you are working with, as well as the locals who are hosting you.

This Before/During/After model will work best if you do the following:

■ *Look for opportunities to learn about yourself, your youth group, your God, and your world.* This journal walks through the steps of before, during, and after in three dimensions: God and Me, God and Us (meaning your youth group), and God and the Locals (meaning the people you serve and those who live in the host community).

■ *Move past service to true justice work.* Justice is working to right wrongs around you. Here's one way to think about the difference between service and justice: You *serve* when you give food to people in need, and you *engage in justice* when you address why people don't have the food they need. Then you work with those people to change the situation so they can get the food they need in the future. We want to help you dive past service into the deeper, and often murkier, waters of justice—into places where you can find lasting solutions to systemic problems. Our prayer is that this journal helps you and your friends dig deeper into the injustices around you so you can unearth the hope and freedom of the gospel.

■ *Schedule time before, during, and after your work to write, draw, and doodle in this journal.* Look at your calendar and see if you can find fifteen minutes here or half an hour there to focus on this journal. If you're doing your work with a team, ask your team leader to set up some specific meetings for your team for that purpose as well.

We are thrilled to navigate this journey into service, compassion, mission, and justice with you. We're praying that God will use this to change your life and the lives of lots of others who are a lot like you!

PART ONE

BEFORE: FRAMING

Get your heart, mind, body, and soul ready
for all that awaits you on your journey.

WHY GO?

BIG IDEA

There are a lot of reasons youth ministries engage in service projects, mission trips, and other kinds of justice work. Early on in the experience, it's a good idea to determine exactly why we're going and to state that reason in one clear sentence we can share with others.

THINK ABOUT THIS

You probably do things every day that you don't put much thought into. You might call them "no-brainers"—you just do them, seemingly without even thinking—for example, brushing your teeth, putting on deodorant (hopefully!), breathing, and tying your shoes. Write a couple of no-brainers here:

_____

_____

_____

_____

Service projects and mission work shouldn't be no-brainers, though.

So here's a big question: *Why am I going?*

DO THIS

In the space below, list all the reasons you can think of for why you're going on this trip. Then circle what you think are the one or two main reasons.

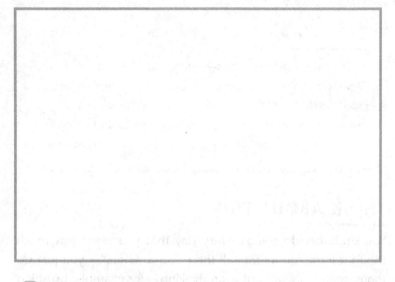

 How do you think the people who will host you might feel about these motives?

 Are there ways you could be more sensitive to the reasons God might want you to be involved in this work?

 Why are you going *together with others* on this trip?

THINK ABOUT THIS

While we often focus on our personal relationships with Jesus, the Bible indicates that the ways we relate to one another are also important.

READ THIS

Matthew 5:13–16 and Matthew 28:16–20

The verbs in this passage are all plural—they imply "you all" together, not just "you" individually. How does that change the way you think about the relevance of these verses for your service?

Now think about how you might summarize the "best" reason for your trip in one sentence.

We're going to _____
                    (place)

to _____
    (what we think we're going to do there)

because _____.
           (why we feel compelled to go)

PRAY

Thank God for the opportunity to serve and bring justice, inviting God to direct your work and your motives with kingdom vision and purpose.

STICKING TOGETHER IN UNITY

BIG IDEA

When we are part of a unified body, we are more open to the work of God's Spirit *in* us and more able to allow Christ to work *through* us as we serve others.

 What are some of the differences that tend to divide people in your school, family, community, country, and world?

 Why do you think it is so difficult for people to see past those differences and be unified?

 What are some of the differences among your mission team members?

THINK ABOUT THIS:

Jesus seemed to care a lot about unity among his disciples, as well as among those who would follow him in the future. In the Scripture passage you're about to read, Jesus has just told the disciples he is about to be arrested and crucified. He's praying for all his disciples—both then and now (which means he's praying for you!).

READ THIS

John 17:20–23

DO THIS

Draw an image of what unity looks like to you.

What are some ways you can seek to be unified with your team during your service project?

PRAY

Read the following prayer for unity, pausing every few lines to reflect and pray over its phrases (if you can, read it aloud with another team member or your whole team):

> *God, we thank you for creating us*
> *to be in relationship with one another.*
> *We confess we often do our own thing,*
> *seek our own interests,*
> *and miss the blessing*
> *of sharing in unity with one another.*
> *Help us depend on you*
> *and offer ourselves to one another.*
> *Unify this team, Lord,*
> *and make us a witness*
> *to your love for the world.*
> *Let your Spirit work in us*
> *and through us as we serve.*
> *Amen.*

WHAT DO THEY NEED MORE?

BIG IDEA

The gospel invites us to focus on people holistically and participate in kingdom work that serves both spiritual and other (physical, relational, economic) needs.

DO THIS

Quickly list some of your own needs this week—big or small.

 As you think about the people you will be serving, what would you guess are some of their needs?

Do you think their biggest need will be to hear or learn more about Jesus or to receive some tangible physical support? Why?

READ THIS

Mark 2:1–12

Does Jesus choose to help this man's soul or his body?

Do you think there's any significance to the fact that Jesus forgave his sins first, before healing him? Why or why not?

THINK ABOUT THIS

You've been thinking about two types of needs—physical and spiritual. Most people tend to think of these needs as completely unrelated, or even as if they were on opposite ends of a continuum.

PHYSICAL/PRACTICAL NEEDS   SPIRITUAL NEEDS

As you see from Jesus' interaction with the paralytic, Jesus doesn't see these two types of needs as separate or in opposition to each other. The reality is that God's kingdom helps meet both types of needs. Instead of a line, God's kingdom is more like a circle.

PHYSICAL NEEDS   SPIRITUAL NEEDS

THINK ABOUT THIS

Jesus' death on the cross is the ultimate example of the gospel's power to meet all our needs. His death not only rescued our souls but also impacts our entire lives—including our relationships, our bodies, and our emotions.

We are kingdom people who are called to follow Jesus' example. The Bible calls that *justice*—following Jesus' example of righting wrongs around us whether they be spiritual, physical, emotional, or all of the above.

In the left circle below, write ways that your upcoming work will impact people's souls.

In the right circle, write ways your upcoming work will impact the rest of their lives.

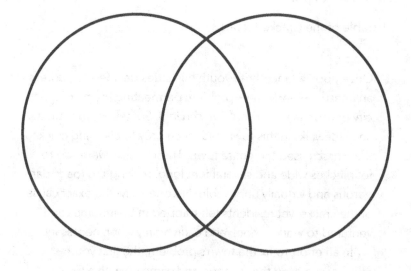

PARABLE OF THE CRACKED ROADS

BIG IDEA

Beyond simply meeting immediate physical needs, justice invites deeper, more holistic, and more systemic solutions.

READ THIS

Parable of the Cracked Roads[2]

Once upon a time, three youth ministries decided to address an unusual—and dire—problem permeating [*name of the city or town in which you'll be serving*]. Somehow, the streets and sidewalks in this town had fallen prey to alarming cracks that crisscrossed the entire town. These cracks were two to four inches wide and several feet long, making the roads dangerous and virtually undrivable. No one knew the exact cause of the cracks, yet residents felt trapped in their homes and ventured to work, school, and church only when necessary.

In an effort to fix the town's problem, the first youth ministry surveyed the damage and came up with a Quick-and-Easy Physical Solution. Their plan was to use a thin layer of topcoat to cover the cracks and render the roads drivable and the sidewalks walkable. Residents stood and watched as the adult leaders and students poured out of their minivans, mixed up the topcoat, and spread it across the cracks like a layer of chocolate icing on a cake. Pleased with the quick repair, the townfolk hugged the young people and cheered as the youth ministry drove off in minivans.

The topcoat worked.

For a few weeks.

But the weight of the cars, the heat of the sun, and the pounding of the rain soon eroded the topcoat. The cracks reappeared, and residents retreated again to their homes. Some thought the cracks were not as severe as they'd been before the topcoat, but no one could be sure.

The second youth ministry, after examining the town's broken roads, adopted a different strategy. Recognizing that there was a lot they didn't know, the students figured they'd better learn more about the town's needs and neighbors before making things right. They divided up into teams, some interviewing the residents and others visiting home improvement stores to learn about the type of cement that would best address the problem.

The neighbors had ideas for road repairs that the youth ministry never would have thought of. As a result, the youth ministry was able to develop a Warm-and-Fuzzy Friendly Solution in which the youth ministry and the neighbors worked side by side filling in the cracks with a customized cement.

The cement worked. For six whole months. But then, to the students' dismay, a new series of cracks began to crisscross the roads. Their new friends told them that even though the Warm-and-Fuzzy Friendly Solution had fixed the old cracks, an entirely new set of cracks had emerged, making the roads almost as hazardous.

The third youth ministry, having heard about the first two well-intentioned-but-failed strategies, knew that neither topcoat nor a brand-new cement would make things right. Like those in the second youth ministry, these students spent several days interviewing neighbors and hearing stories and dreams about crack-free driving as well as the pain and fear caused by the unsafe conditions. Wanting to avoid the mistakes of the first two youth ministries, the third youth ministry adopted a more radical repair strategy.

The students decided to divide into two teams. The first team was tasked with repairing the current cracks. Recognizing that the very foundation of the city's roads was not right, the team members worked with their new friends to jackhammer large sections of road, dig up the resulting rubble, relevel the foundations, and then lay a brand-new asphalt surface for the roads.

In order to prevent the cracks from reappearing, the second team investigated a few deeper and more complex questions. First, the students looked into why the faulty roads had been built in the first place and lobbied at City Hall to change the construction code so defective roads would never be built again. Second, they asked the local people why they'd been unable to fix the roads and then raised funds to provide the training in construction and asphalt-laying that their neighbors would need to keep the roads shipshape in the future.

This Deeper Solution did the trick. Thanks to the new, stable foundation and the neighbors' new training, the broken roads were fixed—for good.

Chances are your goal in this mission isn't to fix cracked roads, so let's translate this parable to what you *will* be doing. What are the immediate physical needs of the people you will be serving? How will you try to meet those needs?

Let's think about some deeper needs of the people you will be serving. What are their emotional, relational, educational, spiritual, and/or economic needs? What deeper structural problems might have led to those needs?

What might be preventing the locals from meeting those needs themselves?

What, if anything, could you do to meet those needs?

THINK ABOUT THIS

One way to think about the difference between service and justice is that we *serve* when we give water to people in need; we *engage in justice* when we figure out why those people don't have the water they need in the first place and then work with those individuals and communities so they have access to clean water in the future.

Another way to say that might be, "Serve the need, and help solve the problem." Both actions are important, and they are dependent on each other.

Often this kind of justice is known as "social justice" because it's about addressing systemic societal issues.

> What would it look like if your goal wasn't to meet the needs of the locals but to help them discover ways to meet their own needs?

> Chances are you won't be able to finish—or maybe even start—the Deeper Solution during your actual time serving. How does that make you feel?

> What, if anything, can you do once you're back home to help the locals keep making progress toward a deeper solution?

The word *justice* might be a new addition to your vocabulary, but we're hoping you learn to use it and fully embrace it, even if it feels unfamiliar at first.

PRAY

In the box below, write or draw your own parable of deeper justice in the community you'll be serving. When you're done, share with God your thoughts, feelings, insights, and deepest dreams for justice.

PRAYER PARTNER GUIDE

BIG IDEA

We need a support network to do this work. Hopefully that includes a prayer partner who meets with us before and after our trip.

THINK ABOUT THIS

Chances are good you have adults in your life (parents and others) who care about you. Your journey will be deeper if you ask one or more of these adults to pray for and maybe even mentor you. Think about adults who will listen well, ask good questions, and support you when you're struggling.

Write down a few possible names here:

DO THIS

Ask your prayer partner to meet with you a few times both before and after your service work (check with your trip leader to see if there will be any planned times for participants and prayer partners to meet as a group). Consider using some of the questions below as springboards for your conversations together.

Questions for both of you to answer:

1. Tell me your story. What's important for me to know about who you are, where you've been, and what God is doing in your life?

2. How do other people describe you, or what do you think your friends would say about you if I asked them to describe you?

3. Read John 15:1–5. What does it look like practically to "remain" in Christ from day to day? What do you think it might look like on this trip?

4. Read Micah 6:8 together. When you think of what God requires of believers, what comes to mind? Does the list in Micah seem like "enough"? Does it seem like "too much"? What are some ways you might act justly, love mercy, and walk humbly with God through this mission experience?

5. Read Luke 9:21–27 together. What do you think it means to take up your cross every day to follow Jesus? What do you think it means for you at your school or at home or at your job? What do you think it might mean during your service work? How do you feel about being asked to make sacrifices for the sake of Christ?

Questions for the trip participant to answer:

1. What draws you to be part of this team/experience? What is it you're hoping for or anticipating from this experience?

2. What do you think life is like in the place you're visiting? How do you think it might be different from—or the same as—life here? If you were growing up there, how might you be different? How does that make you feel?

3. What do you fear about this project? Where do you think those fears are coming from? What do you tend to do when you're afraid? How can I pray for you about your fears?

4. How do you hope to be changed by your work? How do you hope others will be changed?

5. How can I pray for you? What are a few specific things I can pray for as you prepare for the trip? What are the ways I should pray for you during the trip? How can I pray for you when you come home? How do you think I can pray for your family?

WHERE I COME FROM

BIG IDEA

Before we attempt to serve in another cultural context, it's important to "culturally locate" ourselves.

In many ways, culture is like the social air you breathe: Most of the time you don't notice it much and probably don't think about it too hard, but it deeply shapes the ways you think about yourself, others, God, and pretty much everything else! Families are a great example. The way we approach relationships and traditions can be vastly different from one home to the next on the same block.

THINK ABOUT THIS

As you prepare to interact with people from a culture that may be different from yours, it's a good idea to look at your own cultural location—the ways *where you are from* shapes *who you are.* When someone asks where you're from, what do you say?

DO THIS

Here are some prompts that will help you think about who you are and how your background shapes you:

- I was born in ...
- I have lived in ...
- My family is made up of ...
- My parents grew up in ...
- My ancestors came from ...
- I describe my race/ethnicity as ...
- My house/apartment is like ...
- My parents work as ...
- My family likes to eat ...
- My favorite food is ...
- I spend most of my time ...
- When I can choose, I usually spend my free time ...
- My favorite place to go is ...
- The music I listen to is ...
- The clothes I wear are ...
- My clothes come from ...
- I spend money on ...
- I get money from ...

How does your story affect the ways you interact with others who are different?

What are some important things you might want to learn about the cultural location of the people you will serve among during your work?

PRAY

God, I thank you that you've made me. As I interact with people who are different from me, please help me ... [finish in your own words].

BONUS

If you were to draw a map of your life, what might it look like? Think about the geography of your family, your beliefs, the places you've lived, the events and people significant in shaping you, and draw a map that shows the forces that have made you who you are today.

FINDING OURSELVES IN GOD'S STORY

BIG IDEA

We find our ultimate motivation for justice when we find our place in God's story.

THINK ABOUT THIS

Sometimes it's hard for us to make a connection between our everyday lives and the bigger picture of what God is doing in the world. We might wonder whether there's really any significant part for us to play in God's story. Imagine thinking of Scripture as one big story about God's love for the world and the joy God experiences as you and others serve in his kingdom. Here's one way to imagine it:

1. Good

The story starts ... well ... in the beginning. In the first chapter of Genesis, we learn that we were created special, that we were created in God's image, which means that we were created *good*.

> Then God said, "Let us make mankind in our image, in our likeness, so that they may rule over the fish in the sea and the birds in the sky, over the livestock and all the wild animals, and over all the creatures that move along the ground."
>
> So God created mankind in his own image,
>> in the image of God he created them;
>> male and female he created them.
>
> *Genesis 1:26–27*

2. Guilt

Now comes the bad news. Our inherent goodness from being created in God's image has been marred by what happened in the first garden when humans chose to disobey God. All of us have been tainted by *guilt* because of sin, and it impacts us every day.

> There is no one righteous, not even one;
>> there is no one who understands;
>> there is no one who seeks God.
> All have turned away,
>> they have together become worthless;
> there is no one who does good,
>> not even one.
>
> *Romans 3:10–12*

3. Grace

Through the life, death, and resurrection of Jesus, God has extended grace to us to make things right and restore us to relationship with God and one another. It all comes as gift, not something we earn.

> And God raised us up with Christ and seated us with him in the heavenly realms in Christ Jesus, in order that in the coming ages he might show the incomparable riches of his grace, expressed in his kindness to us in Christ Jesus. For it is by grace you have been saved, through faith—and this is not from yourselves, it is the gift of God—not by works, so that no one can boast. For we are God's handiwork, created in Christ Jesus to do good works, which God prepared in advance for us to do.
>
> *Ephesians 2:6–10*

4. God's People

As we experience grace, we are adopted into the body of Christ, embodying God's reign in the world. We join the mission of God, participating in the work of God happening through God's people.

> Consequently, you are no longer foreigners and strangers, but fellow citizens with God's people and also members of his household, built on the foundation of the apostles and prophets, with Christ Jesus himself as the chief cornerstone. In him the whole building is joined together and rises to become a holy temple in the Lord. And in him you too are being built together to become a dwelling in which God lives by his Spirit.
>
> *Ephesians 2:19–22*

5. Gratitude

The grace God offers prompts us to want to serve God out of *gratitude* for all he has done for us. Our lives become like big thank-you notes back to God. As we grow in trust, we naturally grow in obedience as a response to grace.

> So then, just as you received Christ Jesus as Lord, continue to live your lives in him, rooted and built up in him, strengthened in the faith as you were taught, and overflowing with thankfulness.   *Colossians 2:6–7*

6. God's Vision

Now we are living in between Christ's first coming and his second coming, when he will make everything new. Service work and the ways we seek justice on behalf of the poor and oppressed are part of the in-between story that God's kingdom is growing right in front of us. We get to participate in something Jesus has started and that ultimately Jesus will finish.

> Then I saw "a new heaven and a new earth," for the first heaven and the first earth had passed away, and there was no longer any sea. I saw the Holy City, the new Jerusalem, coming down out of heaven from God, prepared as a bride beautifully dressed for her husband. And I heard a loud voice from the throne saying, "Look! God's dwelling place is now among the people, and he will dwell with them. They will be his people, and God himself will be with them and be their God. 'He will wipe every tear from their eyes. There will be no more death' or mourning or crying or pain, for the old order of things has passed away."
>
> He who was seated on the throne said, "I am making everything new!"   *Revelation 21:1–5*

DO THIS

Consider your upcoming project and how the movements in God's story relate to your work. How does the story shape what you hope for as you serve? How does it change the way you serve?

WRITE THIS

What words, questions, and prayers would you like to express to God as you reflect on God's story and what it means for your life and this trip?

BIG IDEA

We reach our full potential in the body of Christ when we work with others, using our unique gifts alongside the gifts Christ has given other followers.

READ THIS

1 Corinthians 12:4–6. Now rewrite these verses in your own words:

 If we really believe the Spirit distributes the various gifts and talents we all have, how should that affect the way we work together?

READ THIS

1 Corinthians 12:7

 Many people refer to the gifts and talents Paul describes in this verse as "spiritual gifts." Remembering that Paul emphasizes that these gifts are to be used for the common good, how would you define "spiritual gifts"?

READ THIS

1 Corinthians 12:8–11

 Which of these gifts do you think you, or someone else in your group, might have? (If you have time, also look at the lists in Romans 12:3–8 and Ephesians 4:11–13.) What other kinds of gifts do you have that are also valuable?

 How do you think these gifts can help you work better together as the body of Christ in your service work?

 If you're not sure what your gifts are, how can your upcoming work give you a better sense of what they might be?

PRAY

Write a prayer next to the gift below. Offer God your gifts, invite God to show you new gifts, and ask for God's help to recognize the gifts of others while you serve.

MISSING HALF THE STORY

BIG IDEA

True partnership means understanding the ministry strategy of the people in our host community.

THINK ABOUT THIS

If you're like most people, you hate it when you get to a movie late and miss the first few minutes. You're likely to feel behind and wonder if you're going to be able to understand the rest of the movie.

In a similar way, the people you are serving are already living out their own stories. After all, they have their own lives, relationships, joys, and struggles, and they are part of the common story of that church or community. You are stepping into their stories—and those are stories that have been running for a long time.

What questions would you want to ask the locals about their story?

God is constantly at work all over the world. What questions would you want to ask about how God is at work in our hosts' community and through their ministry?

 Given your answers to these questions, what commitments would you like to make regarding understanding the locals' stories?

PART TWO

DURING:
EXPERIENCE &
REFLECTION

Catch your breath once or twice each day to pay
attention to the insights emerging from your journey.

DAILY JOURNAL

BIG IDEA

Ongoing reflection on a few simple questions can give a sense of God's activity in the midst of our service.

WRITE ABOUT THIS

Choose two to three questions from the list below and answer them in the space provided on the next page. Then come back another day and answer a couple of other questions, then ... You get the idea. Use this as much as you'd like!

- What was most life giving for you today?

- What was most draining, frustrating, or overwhelming today?

- How are you being stretched?

- How did you experience Christ today? Where did you see God at work?

- What person or experience was most significant for you today? Why?

- For what are you most thankful right now?

DAILY JOURNAL

DAILY JOURNAL

BIG IDEA

Ongoing reflection on a few simple questions can give a sense of God's activity in the midst of our service.

WRITE ABOUT THIS

Choose two to three questions from the list below and answer them in the space provided on the next page. Then come back another day and answer a couple of other questions, then ... You get the idea. Use this as much as you'd like!

- What was most life giving for you today?
- What was most draining, frustrating, or overwhelming today?
- How are you being stretched?
- How did you experience Christ today? Where did you see God at work?
- What person or experience was most significant for you today? Why?
- For what are you most thankful right now?

DAILY JOURNAL

DAILY JOURNAL

BIG IDEA

Ongoing reflection on a few simple questions can give a sense of God's activity in the midst of our service.

WRITE ABOUT THIS

Choose two to three questions from the list below and answer them in the space provided on the next page. Then come back another day and answer a couple of other questions, then ... You get the idea. Use this as much as you'd like!

- What was most life giving for you today?
- What was most draining, frustrating, or overwhelming today?
- How are you being stretched?
- How did you experience Christ today? Where did you see God at work?
- What person or experience was most significant for you today? Why?
- For what are you most thankful right now?

DAILY JOURNAL

DAILY JOURNAL

BIG IDEA

Ongoing reflection on a few simple questions can give a sense of God's activity in the midst of our service.

WRITE ABOUT THIS

Choose two to three questions from the list below and answer them in the space provided on the next page. Then come back another day and answer a couple of other questions, then ... You get the idea. Use this as much as you'd like!

- What was most life giving for you today?
- What was most draining, frustrating, or overwhelming today?
- How are you being stretched?
- How did you experience Christ today? Where did you see God at work?
- What person or experience was most significant for you today? Why?
- For what are you most thankful right now?

DAILY JOURNAL

DURING: GOD AND ME
DAILY JOURNAL

BIG IDEA

Ongoing reflection on a few simple questions can give a sense of God's activity in the midst of our service.

WRITE ABOUT THIS

Choose two to three questions from the list below and answer them in the space provided on the next page. Then come back another day and answer a couple of other questions, then ... You get the idea. Use this as much as you'd like!

- What was most life giving for you today?
- What was most draining, frustrating, or overwhelming today?
- How are you being stretched?
- How did you experience Christ today? Where did you see God at work?
- What person or experience was most significant for you today? Why?
- For what are you most thankful right now?

DAILY JOURNAL

DURING: GOD AND ME

YOUR KINGDOM COME

BIG IDEA

The prayer Jesus taught his followers can be more than just some traditional words you recite—it can help us see God's will being done through our lives.

 What things did you see in the past day or so that made you want to pray, or when did you find yourself praying about something you saw or experienced?

READ THIS

Matthew 6:9–13

WRITE THIS

Which phrase in the prayer is most meaningful to you right now? Write that phrase below, and then spend some time doodling, sketching, or sitting still and reflecting on that prayer and all it means for your life as well as the people in the community you're serving. Talk to God as you do.

 How could this prayer lead you to action today?

REMAINING IN CHRIST

BIG IDEA

We can only do God's kingdom work by remaining connected to Christ.

READ THIS

John 15:1–5

Pruning is necessary for the health of the vine. Dead wood is worse than fruitlessness because it has the potential for increased disease and decay. An untrimmed vine will grow long, rambling branches that produce little fruit.

THINK OR WRITE ABOUT THIS:

"Remaining in" Jesus means depending on him. What are some ways you can remain in or depend on Jesus during your work on this trip?

What kind of fruit do you think Jesus is talking about?

 What type of fruit have you already seen in the midst of your work?

PRAY

Jesus said, "I am the vine; you are the branches. If you remain in me and I in you, you will bear much fruit; apart from me you can do nothing" (John 15:5). In light of these words, complete the following prayer (you can write or just pray silently):

Jesus, I confess that I have not always remained in you ...

Please help me to remain in you by ...

Please give me wisdom so I might know ...

Please empower me by your grace so I can ...

DURING: GOD AND ME
PRAYER OF REVIEW

BIG IDEA

God is constantly present with us. From time to time we can stop and prayerfully review God's presence in our lives and even the way he shows up through others.

THINK ABOUT THIS

In order to help you sift through the noise of the day's experiences and become more aware of how Christ has been present, please take the next few minutes to walk through a prayer of review.[3]

PRAY

Take a moment now to stop, to become still and focused.

Let your breathing help you relax as you breathe in and out.

As you begin the prayer, ask God to guide your thoughts, feelings, and reactions so you might see God's presence in your life.

And now begin to recall the day:

How did you feel when you woke up this morning and during the first part of the day?

What was happening?

What sort of mood or moods were you in?

How did you spend your morning and the middle of the day?

Whom were you with?

What was happening?

Now let your memory drift over your afternoon and evening, recalling events, people, and places.

With whom did you most connect? Why do you think that was?

How were you feeling at different times? Try to name for yourself the different moods you felt.

As you consider your whole day, when did you notice times of light or life?

What gifts have you received today?

Take a moment to relish these gifts and give thanks to God for them.

If there have been difficult times or difficult people, notice them too, offering them to God that he may send his grace and love into them.

When have you known God today?

When have you seen Christ in others?

Take a moment to talk to God as you would to a friend about your day. You can write a prayer here if you'd like.

As this day comes toward its end and you look forward to the next, is there anything you want to ask of God for the coming day(s)? Take a moment to do this before you bring your prayer to a close.

 What things did God reveal to you during the prayer? Share with someone on your trip!

ENGAGING OUR SENSES

BIG IDEA

Stopping to notice the sights, sounds, and objects around us can give us new insights into others and ourselves.

THINK ABOUT THIS

Taking the time to think about the things we're observing is an important part of learning from our work. This practice can give us clues about our experience and can raise important questions about our host community that we need to ask others.

DRAW THIS

One image of the local community where you're serving that sticks out to you most. It might be a person, a home, a tree, a road—anything that's stuck in your head like a snapshot.

WRITE THIS

Complete the following sentences:

The main sound I hear is _____.

One smell I've noticed here is _____.

Something I haven't seen here is _____.

Something I see that looks a lot like home is _____.

People's primary tasks here seem to be _____.

The most common objects I see are _____.

The teenagers here are _____.

 What did you notice about the types of things you wrote down? Were there any themes?

 How well do you think you really know this place and these people? How can you go deeper? Whom could you ask for help?

 Based on what you have observed, how can you approach this culture and these people more effectively?

PRAY

God, thank you for teaching me more about other people and another culture. Please give me eyes to see new things about this community and new ways I can be involved in serving and seeking justice here.

WHY ASK "WHY?"

BIG IDEA

Truly meeting the needs of the poor means pushing beyond immediate help and asking why they are poor in the first place.

WRITE THIS:

 In what ways have you encountered or experienced poverty before this experience?

 What did you see, smell, or hear today that reflected a sense of poverty among the people we met?

When you encounter people who are poor, how do you feel? What do you tend to think about? What did you think about today?

THINK ABOUT THIS

Dom Hélder Câmara was a twentieth-century Roman Catholic priest who showed a relentless commitment to justice work among the poor of Brazil. Câmara is famous for the following quotation:

> When I feed the poor, they call me a saint.

> When I ask why the poor have no food, they call me a communist.[4]

 How would you restate Câmara's quotation in your own words?

 What do you agree with in this quotation? What do you disagree with?

 If Câmara walked up to Jesus and said these two sentences to him, what do you think Jesus would say in response?

THINK ABOUT THIS

Sometimes Christians divide over whether it's more important to make a personal decision to follow Jesus or to do more to help the poor in Jesus' name. We'd have a much deeper understanding of both sides of the kingdom if we grasped God's plan for his creation. Since the beginning of time, God has wanted to establish *shalom* over all his people and all creation.

Shalom is a Hebrew word often translated as "peace," and while that's not a bad translation, we've tended to focus on only a few angles of the peace God intends. We often think of peace as an absence of conflict or some warm-and-fuzzy feeling that everything is going to work out okay. *Shalom* is far more than that. The type of peace God intends has many forms:

- Peace with God
- Peace with nature
- Peace with other humans
- Peace with oneself[5]

⊘ How, if at all, does that sense of expanded *shalom* relate to Dom Hélder Câmara's quotation?

⊘ Based on what we've just discussed, how would you like to deepen our service and justice work in ...

- the next twenty-four hours?

- the next week?

- the next month?

"IF YOU'RE HAPPY AND YOU KNOW IT ... SMILE."

BIG IDEA

When we encounter poverty, we're faced with the challenging task of thinking about the connection between material possessions and happiness in our own lives and in the lives of those we serve.

THINK ABOUT THIS

Short-term mission experiences often bring people into contact with situations of extreme poverty, sometimes for the first time. Consider this common statement that has been made by members of short-term teams who encounter poverty: *"These people are so happy despite the horrid conditions in which they live. They sing with joy, they serve us better meals than they eat themselves, and they are so content."*

How does this statement relate to your own thoughts and experiences during your trip?

Can you think of a time when you felt extremely content and it had nothing to do with money or the things you had? If so, why did you feel content then?

It's been said that true contentment can come only to a person who has a relationship with Jesus Christ. Do you agree or not? Explain.

Since you are a visitor to this community, take some time to think about your own experiences when people come to visit you. How might the emotions you show when someone visits your house or community be similar to the emotions your hosts are showing toward you and your team?

THINK ABOUT THIS

Just as you and your family might become more positive when guests walk into your home and lives, the locals might be doing the same thing.

If you assume people are "happy" because they smile at you during your visit, how might that affect your commitment to seeking justice?

DRAW THIS

A picture of someone you've met during your service. Next to or below the picture, write what you think Jesus would like to say to them in the midst of the ups and downs of their life.

LISTENING TO LOCAL HOSTS

BIG IDEA

We have the huge privilege of building relationships with our local hosts by listening.

READ THIS

The statements that follow (most of which are actual quotations) contrast the reflections of North Americans who travel to another country on a service project with what locals think:[6]

North Americans	Non–North American Hosts
"We've got to do something. The window of opportunity is *now*! The time for change is ripe. We must seize this opportunity." —a recurring statement made by short-term missions (STM) teams	"You too quickly get into the action without thinking through the implications for our churches long after you go home." —a recurring concern voiced by local believers who receive STM teams

North Americans	Non–North American Hosts
"They're dirt poor. It just makes me realize how blessed I am to be born in America." —one of the most common statements made by STM teams. It's usually combined with a statement about the happiness of the poor people encountered	"I can still feel like a stranger in the American church, especially when short-termers return from India bubbling over their accomplishments and describing my birthplace as a land of deprivation." — a comment from an Indian-American woman on the ways STM teams obsess over the poverty of places visited
"It felt really good to work so hard. We gave them some buildings they never would have had without us being there." —a recurring statement made by STM teams	"I found out soon enough that I was in the way. The group wanted to do things their way and made me feel like I didn't know what I was doing. I only helped the first day." —a comment from a Honduran bricklayer who planned to help a team build houses for hurricane victims

 What quotations in this chart might feel similar to things you are thinking or saying as you serve? How are you and/ or your team acting or talking differently?

What kinds of things can you do to avoid seeming like the people quoted above?

76

In many cultures people would be too embarrassed to tell you explicitly if you're being offensive. So you have to watch for cues. As you interact with the locals here, what clues would tell you that you are being sensitive and honoring to them? What clues might tell you you're not?

What can you do tomorrow to get to know one or two locals better? How specifically can you begin to practice listening well to them?

PRAY

Ask God to help you truly listen to your local hosts during your trip, and ask him to strengthen your relationships with them.

FINDING THE FACE OF CHRIST

BIG IDEA

Serving others allows us to encounter Christ in those we serve, in our teammates, and even in ourselves.

WRITE ABOUT THIS

 How would you describe the faces you've seen in the past day? What words would you use to describe their appearance, emotions, expressions, or reactions?

How would you describe the faces you've seen in the past day? What words would you use to describe their appearance, emotions, expressions, or reactions?

Whose face made you smile? Why do you think you reacted so positively to that person?

Whose face bothered you the most? Why do you think you reacted so strongly?

 Now think about yourself. What do you think others learned about you through your face?

 Now think about that a different way: What do you think others learned about *Christ* through your face in the past day?

READ THIS

Matthew 25:34–40

 Why do you think Jesus was so emphatic that serving people in need is the same thing as serving him?

 Think back to the faces you saw yesterday. How does it make you think differently about them when you consider that those faces were the very face of Christ?

DRAW THIS

Your own face as you served today.

PRAY

Jesus, please help me show you to others during the rest of this trip, and help me see your face in others.

SAYING GOOD-BYE WELL

BIG IDEA

Saying an appropriate good-bye is an important part of our cross-cultural service experience.

THINK ABOUT THIS

In many cultures, the way you say good-bye says a lot about who you are. As we are leaving this service site, to whom do you most need to do a good job of saying good-bye?

Put an X on the line at the spot that best describes how you feel about good-byes.

●────────────────────────────────────●

| I DON'T MIND THEM | I HAVEN'T THOUGHT MUCH ABOUT THEM | I DON'T LIKE THEM |

Write down one moment you remember in which you, or someone you know, didn't say good-bye very well. How did people (including you!) feel when that happened?

READ THIS

Look up the following Scripture verses one at a time and then write down your answers. Each passage reflects a different "good-bye" in the New Testament:

1. Luke 9:61. The word for *good-bye* in this verse means "to dismiss with orders." Write down times when someone might give instructions as part of their good-bye.

2. Philippians 4:4. The word for *rejoice* also was used for *good-bye*. Write down ways a good-bye can be a joyful time.

3. The apostle Paul provides a great example of taking time to say good-bye well. In the midst of his third missionary journey around the Mediterranean, Paul says good-bye to the elders in Ephesus in Acts 20:17 – 38.

 What did Paul remember about his relationship with the Ephesian elders?

 What was Paul's main concern in the present?

How did Paul want them to get ready for the future?

What does Paul model for us in the way he says good-bye?

DRAW THIS

Close your eyes and imagine the people to whom you will have to say good-bye when you leave this place. As you think about the good-byes you'll be saying soon, what words, actions, or attitudes would you like to be part of your good-byes? Draw or write them below.

PART THREE

AFTER: DEBRIEF

Take some time as your work comes to a close to
cement all that you've learned and experienced.

AFTER: DEBRIEF — GOD AND ME

REFLECT BACK

BIG IDEA

We've just experienced a lot. Let's catch our breath and reflect on our trip before the return home.

DO THIS

Flip back through some of your journal entries before and during your work to help you remember some of your most vivid moments. While you do, think about these questions:

 What was this trip like for you?

 Where did you see growth? How were you stretched?

 When did you see God's presence or work? Where did you meet God?

What person or experience was most significant for you and why?

How do you see God differently now? How do you see the world differently? What about how you see yourself has changed?

DRAW THIS

A picture that illustrates from an outside perspective some of your experience during your journey. You might want to draw people you met, places you saw, and things you did that stand out as being significant to you. If you want, you could chart your journey like a map by listing or drawing the experiences that most impacted you from start to finish.

NOW DRAW THIS

Your experience from an internal perspective. In other words, draw about how your experiences made you feel, the new things you learned about, as well as how God shaped or changed your heart. If you'd like, you can also chart your own internal experiences by making a map.

 Did anything surprise you or stand out as you recalled the significant people, places, moments, events, and feelings from your service work?

INITIAL DEBRIEF: SHARING THE HIGHLIGHTS

BIG IDEA

Sharing your experience right away helps you process what you've learned and lets others know what God is doing.

THINK ABOUT THIS

The transition back home from your mission trip is difficult in many ways, but sometimes the hardest part is figuring out how to share it with others who haven't lived it with you. Here are three different ways you can share about your journey. Use the boxes provided to write your thoughts.

The Thirty-Second Highlight:[7] When people ask the quick question, "How was your trip?" in passing, don't just settle for typical quick responses like "Good" or "It was fun." Think of a two- or three-sentence response that will tell them about something significant you learned or someone significant you met. Your thirty-second response might even spark their interest and cause them to ask more questions!

The Three-Minute Highlight: You may be asked to share about your mission experience at youth group, a family gathering, over a meal, or even in a class. If you have only a couple of minutes, it's better to share one meaningful moment or story and what God taught you through it than to rush through all the details of the entire trip or event.

The Whole Enchilada: Everybody needs at least one opportunity to unload all the details, emotions, funny highlights, and meaningful memories of their service experience. We encourage you to find at least two people (an adult and a friend your age) who were not with you on the trip and invite them into your experience by telling them your highlights and showing them your pictures.

Sharing about how your views of God, yourself, and others were changed during your work will help you process your experience and also help those close to you understand how you've been impacted by the experience. It may even help them to see the world, themselves, and God in new ways.

Note: You probably can't write about everything here and now, but you can jot down a few words or names that you want to remember to share about later.

PRAY THIS

God, when I have chances to share about my trip, please help me to ... [complete the prayer with your own words].

SHARING THE JOURNEY

BIG IDEA

Learning to share what we've experienced is helpful not only for our team but also for others back home.

THINK ABOUT THIS

Right now you're probably talking about experiences with others who shared them with you on the trip. But as you transition home, you will be sharing your experiences with others who didn't take part in the experience. That can be hard. Think about what you want to share about what you learned on this journey, and write some of your ideas here:

 What did you learn about yourself during your journey?

What new things did you learn about God?

What did you learn from people in the community?

 Who/what do you specifically want to pray for after you return home?

 How are you a different person now compared to when you signed up for this work?

 How do you want our youth group to be involved in service at home? How do you want to be personally involved in serving or seeking justice?

AFTER: DEBRIEF—GOD AND US

BACK TO THE "REAL WORLD"

BIG IDEA

On cross-cultural trips, we often see the "real world" in ways we've never seen it, including the *real* truth about poverty or glimpses of the *real* kingdom of God. This is the "real world" of following Jesus that we can continue to live out every day.

What have you missed about your life at home while you've been away?

We often refer to life back home as the "real world." Why do we call it that?

If you asked Jesus which of your worlds (the world where you've been serving or the world back home) is the "real world," what do you think he would say?

In what ways have you seen the "real" church as you've served, either among your team or among the local people?

THINK ABOUT THIS

Justice work can sometimes give you a different idea of what it really means to follow Jesus and be part of the kingdom community. If that happens, you have at least three potential responses:

>> **CONSUME.** You can go home with a couple of cheap souvenirs and say to yourself, "What happens in _____ [location] stays in _____ [location]." You can forget how God spoke to you in the midst of your time there and go back to your life as if nothing happened.

>> **CONDEMN.** You can get angry about the way your friends, family, and church all seem stuck in their old ways and just don't seem to "get it."

>> **CREATE.** You can go home and find ways to get involved in kingdom service in your own backyard. You can choose to create a community that's centered on mission and stay involved in righting wrongs so God's kingdom is made clearer.

How do you think you're most likely to respond to life back at home?

 What would it take for you to help create more of a missional community at home?

DRAW OR WRITE THIS

How have you seen the "real world" of following Jesus as you've served?

DRAW OR WRITE THIS

How would you like to live out the Jesus-focused "real world" you've seen as you transition home?

WHO'S MY NEIGHBOR?

BIG IDEA

We can share with people in our own schools and community the same love we lived out during our trip.

THINK ABOUT THIS

Flying overseas or driving away from home to serve in a different community can be exhilarating. It's easy to fall in love with people for a few days in the midst of the excitement of service and justice work.

Coming back home to the people in our own neighborhoods isn't quite as glamorous. But we don't live out the gospel primarily in faraway places a couple of weeks a year. We live out the gospel 24/7 with the people at school, at home, and in the neighborhood.

READ THIS

Luke 10:25–37

The road from Jerusalem to Jericho was about seventeen miles long and curved through rugged terrain with plenty of large rocks for thieves to hide behind. As a result, traveling this road was very dangerous.

Luke 10:27 quotes the Old Testament's commands to love God and love our neighbor. How are those two love commands connected to each other?

How does Jesus define a "neighbor"?

Based on Jesus' definition, who are *your* "neighbors"?

What would it mean to love them as yourself?

THINK ABOUT THIS

It's possible that your trip gave you new opportunities to interact with people whose racial or ethnic background is different from your own. It's worth considering how Jesus' story of the good Samaritan speaks to issues of racism and racial stereotyping. Racism and stereotyping are not new problems. During Jesus' lifetime, both were widespread. For example, most first-century Jews couldn't stand Samaritans. So when Jesus used a Samaritan as the role model for living out the greatest commandments, instead of the priest or Levite, his Jewish audience must have been shocked!

Jesus not only called the Jews to watch out for the wounded and oppressed alongside the road, but he also invited the Jews to love the Samaritans and to realize that they as Jews had something to learn from the Samaritans.

WRITE THIS:

 Who are the "Samaritans" in your life—the people who seem so different that you find it hard to relate to them? Are there certain groups or individuals who make you annoyed or anxious because they feel unfamiliar to you?

 What would it look like for you to love those neighbors as you love yourself this week?

 What impact would loving those people as you love yourself have on the way you love God?

What thoughts, feelings, or prayers come to you right now? Write or sketch them below.

REVERSE CULTURE SHOCK

BIG IDEA

Cross-cultural experiences can create a type of reverse culture shock when we reenter our home environment. We can process those experiences through the lens of God's kingdom-on-earth culture.

THINK ABOUT THIS

You likely noticed some differences between your own culture and the culture in which you recently served. In the columns below, write down words that describe aspects of the two cultures.

	On the Trip	At Home
Airports		
Markets/grocery stores		
Schools		
Restaurants		
Homes		

	On the Trip	At Home
Churches		
Methods of trans-portation		
Roads		
Landscaping		
Shopping areas or malls		
Other differences		

 In what ways do the two cultures differ?

 What are some things the two cultures have in common?

People who travel away from home and experience a new culture often experience "reverse culture shock" when they return home, as elements of their home culture suddenly seem unfamiliar and even strange. What do you think you'll struggle with most in "reverse culture shock"?

103

READ THIS

Read the passage below three times, listening for any words or images that stand out to you.

> So here's what I want you to do, God helping you: Take your everyday, ordinary life—your sleeping, eating, going-to-work, and walking-around life—and place it before God as an offering. Embracing what God does for you is the best thing you can do for him. Don't become so well-adjusted to your culture that you fit into it without even thinking. Instead, fix your attention on God. You'll be changed from the inside out. Readily recognize what he wants from you, and quickly respond to it. Unlike the culture around you, always dragging you down to its level of immaturity, God brings the best out of you, develops well-formed maturity in you.
>
> *Romans 12:1–2 MSG*

What images or experiences came to mind as you read this passage from Romans?

What, if anything, did God say to you?

How can you apply any insights from Romans 12:1–2 to your experience of reverse culture shock?

PRAY

Using phrases or imagery from Romans 12:1–2, write your own prayer to God.

AFTER: DEBRIEF — GOD AND ME

THEN AND NOW

BIG IDEA

The kingdom of God is bigger than we think.

THINK ABOUT THIS

These days there are many television shows and posts that contrast what someone or something was like "then" (before some dramatic transformation) with what they or it is like "now." In many ways we're experiencing our own "then" and "now" during this work.

WRITE THIS

Take a few minutes to complete the following sentences:

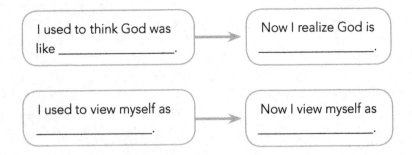

I used to think God was like _____. → Now I realize God is _____.

I used to view myself as _____. → Now I view myself as _____.

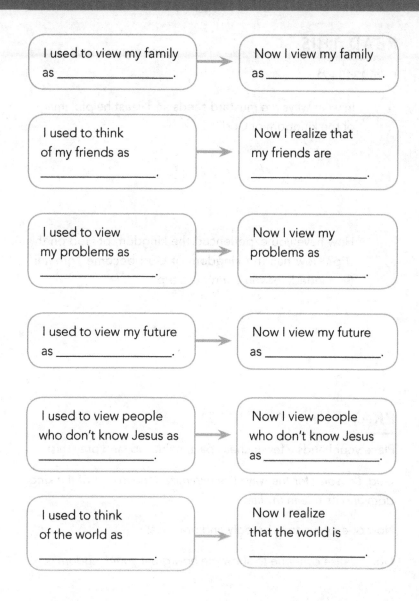

I used to view my family as _____.

→

Now I view my family as _____.

I used to think of my friends as _____.

→

Now I realize that my friends are _____.

I used to view my problems as _____.

→

Now I view my problems as _____.

I used to view my future as _____.

→

Now I view my future as _____.

I used to view people who don't know Jesus as _____.

→

Now I view people who don't know Jesus as _____.

I used to think of the world as _____.

→

Now I realize that the world is _____.

READ THIS

Luke 13:18–21

 In what ways are mustard seeds and yeast helpful images of the kingdom of God?

 How have you experienced the kingdom of God on this trip? How has the kingdom of God become "greater" (expanded) for you during this trip?

PRAY THIS

Place your hands a few inches apart, palms up, and pray this:

God, I'm sorry for the ways I've minimized the power of the king-dom and its role in my life.

Now open your arms broadly and pray this:

God, please continue to show me how great your kingdom is.

PART FOUR

AFTER: ONGOING TRANSFORMATION

Connect the dots between your trip and
daily life for the next several weeks and months.

REENTRY

BIG IDEA

Returning from a short-term mission trip can be difficult and disorienting, but it does not have to paralyze us. We can live differently as a result of our experience!

? What has been the best part of being back home?

? What has been the hardest part about being back home?

THINK ABOUT THIS

Reentry into life back home after a mission trip can sometimes leave you feeling torn. You come home feeling that God has changed you, and you want to live differently because of it. But it can be difficult to figure out how to do that as you enter back into your own culture and old habits.

Here are five common experiences of people returning from a cross-cultural mission experience:[8]

- *Fun:* You like returning to the comforts you enjoy back home.
- *Flee:* You miss your team and struggle to find people you can share your experience with, so you end up feeling lonely and isolated.
- *Fight:* You get frustrated with your own culture's selfishness or indifference and fight against conforming to it.
- *Fit:* You grow tired of fighting and just try to fit back into your own culture.
- *Far:* You experience God as seeming further away than on the trip and wonder whether you left God there in the other culture.

Which of these best describes your reaction(s) right now?

How might you work through this response in a healthy way? Who could you ask for help processing this?

PRAY THIS

God, right now I'm responding to being back home by ...

That makes me feel ...

Please help me to ...

SUGGESTIONS FOR OVERCOMING A ROUGH REENTRY[9]

WRITE ABOUT IT! Journaling helps you sort through your thoughts and feelings and allows you to express them in a healthy way.

TALK ABOUT IT! Find two people you trust, and share your experience with them. Tell them your stories, your hopes, your frustrations—tell them everything—and ask them to pray for you as you translate your experience into your life back home.

DO SOMETHING ABOUT IT! Identify an issue or a need in your own community and do something to address it. If you are concerned with poverty, find out who is working to help impoverished people in your community and volunteer to serve with them.

EMBRACE IT! Incorporating what you have experienced on your mission trip into your everyday life and faith is an ongoing process. It's okay to have doubts, questions, and mixed emotions. Remember that every step of the journey is important, no matter how small.

POST-TRIP PRAYER PARTNER MEETING

BIG IDEA

God shapes us in many ways, including through taking time to process with a trusted adult.

THINK ABOUT THIS

You're back, and you have a *lot* to share. Schedule a time with your prayer partner or another trusted adult mentor who will listen to your story and help you process it. Here are a few questions to think about as you share. (Take this guide with you to your meeting, and maybe even hand this list over to your prayer partner! You don't have to answer every question.) Also bring along some photos of your experience to show your partner as you tell stories. You may actually want to print five to ten photos rather than skimming through lots of digital images together.

1. What one word or phrase would you use to describe your experience?

2. If you could add a few more words or phrases to more fully describe your experience, what would they be?

3. What surprised you? How did that impact your work?

4. What disappointed you? What do you wish had been different about your experience? How did that impact your work?

5. When were you most overwhelmed? What did you do about that, or how did you respond to that feeling?

6. How was life in the place you visited different than you thought it would be? What discoveries did you make?

7. Where did you sense God at work in your life and in the lives of others during this experience?

8. What do you think other people saw in you during your time serving?

9. What has it been like to reenter life with your family and friends at home? What kinds of feelings are you experiencing?

10. How do you see life here differently now? How do you feel about that? Where do you sense God at work here?

11. What do you hope will change about your life as a result of this experience? Who can help you make those changes or hold you accountable for them?

12. How do you hope our church changes as a result of your team's experience?

13. How can you live out justice beyond this particular experience? What dreams do you have for justice both where you visited and here at home?

14. How are you going to talk with others about your work? If you were going to share a thirty-second version of your experience, what would you say?

A PICTURE IS WORTH A LOT OF WORDS

BIG IDEA

There are more connections between our service work and our life at home than we might realize.

DRAW OR WRITE ABOUT THIS

One or two memories from your work that are most vivid.

DRAW OR WRITE ABOUT THIS

Your favorite place to hang out when you're in your own town or city.

 How do these two pictures relate to each other?

 How does your work *there* relate to your life *here and now*?

PRAY THIS

God, as I think about my memories from my work, I feel …

By your grace, please do great work in the lives of the people we served and …

Now that I'm home, please help me to …

REWIND AND FAST-FORWARD

BIG IDEA

A month or two after our work, it's a good idea to rewind time to remind ourselves of how we were impacted, then fast-forward to think about how God is continuing to change us.

THINK ABOUT THIS

God's change process often resembles the way water shapes rock. Let's think for a moment about all the different ways water shapes rock ...

- God's transformation can seem slow at times, as if we're a stone that's being smoothed in a creek.

- Sometimes it can even seem too slow, as if we're just a stone sitting in the middle of a pond and nothing much is happening.

- Or sometimes it seems quick, like a rushing river flowing over stones in its path.

- Other times it seems overwhelming, making us feel vulnerable, like a rock being pelted under a huge waterfall.

119

Which of these images of rock being shaped by water seems to resonate most with the way God's been changing you during and/or since your trip?

 What decisions or commitments did you make during or immediately after your time serving?

 Let's be honest: Which of these decisions or commitments have gone well — and which ones haven't gone so well? Why do you think that is?

 Are there decisions or commitments you'd like to revise based on what life is like now that you're back home?

 Now fast-forward and think about the next month. How do you want to invite God's ongoing transformation into your regular life? What can you do to support other team members in living out that transformation too?

DRAW THIS

A picture that shows what's on your mind or heart right now. Feel free to include rocks and water if you'd like, and if you want to pray, that's good too.

NET WORTH

BIG IDEA

Serving in the kingdom of God reorients our ideas of personal value and net worth.

THINK ABOUT THIS

Remember back to your trip and anything that you can think of related to the ways the people in the community used money or might have used money.

 From what you could tell, how did the locals we served use their money? How is that similar to the way you and your family use it? How is it different?

DO THIS

Figure out how much money is represented at this moment on your person. In other words, what is your "net worth" right now? Make a guess at how much was spent (by you or someone else) on your shoes, jeans, jacket, purse, sunglasses, cell phone, jewelry, whatever is in your backpack or wallet, even your braces, the highlights in your hair ... *anything* you can put a monetary value on. List all this stuff, and add up the total dollar amount: $_____

What, if anything, about your own net worth surprised or shocked you? What questions does it raise, or what does it make you want to do?

How, if at all, is your own willingness to spend money on yourself different from what you would have said before your trip? Why do you think that is?

Whether it's jeans, shoes, or the number of albums you download from iTunes, how do you determine when you've crossed a line into what is "excessive"? As people who want to serve others, when—if ever—is it okay to spend extravagantly on yourself?

Here's a startling reality: US citizens make up only 5 percent of the world's population, but we consume half the world's resources.[10] Given what you've seen in the midst of your service experience, how does that make you feel?

READ THIS

Mark 10:17–27

 This young man clearly had tried to honor God in many ways, but Jesus told him something was missing. How would you describe in your own words what this man was missing?

Note what the rich ruler asks Jesus: "Good teacher, what must I *do* to inherit eternal life?" (v. 17, emphasis added). Ironically, Jesus had just taught in Mark 10:15 that the kingdom is more about *receiving* than *doing*.

 If Jesus told you to do the same thing, how do you think you would respond?

 How can you use what you've been given—your own net worth—in a spirit of extravagant generosity that offers good news to others, especially to the poor?

THINK ABOUT THIS

Reflect on what you value and why. Create a "lowering my net worth" list below—brainstorming ways you can reduce the costly material stuff that clutters your life and then possibly redistribute some of that money and stuff to others.

PRAY

Offer God your ideas and any changes you think the Holy Spirit might be prompting you to make in your spending or your attitudes about having a lot of stuff.

PAYING ATTENTION TO THE PRESENCE OF GOD

BIG IDEA

Practicing spiritual disciplines helps us notice God's activity and experience God's presence in our lives after we return from our trip.

What was your most memorable time of sensing God's presence during your trip?

THINK ABOUT THIS

Sometimes after we come back from doing mission work, we can feel like God's presence seems to disappear. When we were serving, we seemed to experience God's presence so intensely. But when we get home, it can feel like God is far away.

Why do you think it is so much more difficult to experience God's presence once you've returned home?

THINK ABOUT THIS

The reality is that God is always present with us, but we often miss the signs of God's presence in our everyday lives.

READ THIS

The list below and on pages 128–129 describes some common practices that are sometimes called "spiritual disciplines."[11] Underline any you have practiced before. Circle one or two you have never experienced but would like to try.

Meditation. Slowing down and cutting out all the noise around you so you can focus your heart and mind on Jesus.

Prayer. Listening to and talking with God, not just when you fold your hands and close your eyes, but anytime you talk with or just "be" with God.

Study. Searching for the truth of God through Scripture, creation, church tradition, and the wisdom of saints who have gone before you.

Fasting. Abstaining from something and being filled instead by the presence of God. It could mean fasting from food, music, your favorite soft drink, or anything else you use for fulfillment.

Simplicity. Living without being enslaved to your stuff (cars, clothes, gadgets, bling, etc.). Simplicity is about being free from the control of materialism so you can freely give to and receive from others.

Solitude. Being alone and facing your loneliness as you encounter God. Solitude allows you to come face-to-face with God without the comfort or distraction of others.

Submission. Denying yourself, often to give to another, not out of duty but in love and freedom. It can include giving up your power, possessions, comfort, opinions, and even your life for the sake of others.

Service. Humbling yourself and serving the needs of others. Jesus modeled this discipline in washing his disciples' feet.

Confession. Confessing your sins and temptations to another trusted believer. In confession you are able to forgive and bear with one another as you experience God's grace and forgiveness.

Worship. Noticing God's presence and responding to God's grace, beauty, and love. Worship can be expressed in a lot of ways, including silence, song, or creating art.

Guidance. Seeking the wisdom of others for direction in your life and spiritual journey. It involves seeking the guidance of the Holy Spirit through the voice of a faithful community of supporters.

Celebration. Partying! Remember, the gospel literally means "good news"! You have every reason to celebrate God's goodness, enjoy God's creation, and embrace the people God has put in your life.

 Now look back at the spiritual discipline(s) you underlined. What can you do this week to experience God's presence through practicing one or more of these disciplines in a fresh and new way?

 Look at the spiritual discipline(s) you circled. How will you explore those disciplines this week?

Now you're all stirred up. You know more than you did at the start of this journey—maybe a lot more. You've seen needs you hadn't seen before—maybe a lot of needs. You want to do something.

But it can be overwhelming. The needs of the world are big.

How do you take the next step?

Here are a few suggestions and questions to get you started:

1. *View wide, engage deep.* When it comes to world justice issues, we think Christ-followers should be some of the savviest, best-informed people on the planet. But you can't tackle *every* problem. Start with a wide view, then begin to engage deep into something you care about deeply.

What justice issues most resonate with you or stir you up?

What do you know already about what's being done to meet those needs? How can you find out more?

What are some big ideas and dreams you have for serving in response to one or two of those needs?

2. *Pick an issue, pick a place.* The only way we can engage deep is by focusing our efforts carefully. This doesn't mean abandoning all of the world's other needs. It just means choosing to zero in on one issue and one place *for now*.

 What one issue and/or one place (a city, neighborhood, country, or people group) are closest to your heart? If you had to pick somewhere to start, where would that be for now?

 What ideas do you have to make a difference in that one place focused on that one issue?

 Who else can you invite into your planning? What friends might be interested? What adult can you talk to? What family members might want to join you in your efforts?

What do you think is your very next step in this process? Is it more research? A conversation with a leader? Making time to pray?

 When can you get started? Pick a date and set up a time to take your next step!

As you move forward in your journey, may our Lord continue to guide you on your path. As you keep in step with God's kingdom work, the best is yet to be!

EXTRA JOURNALING

EXTRA JOURNALING

EXTRA JOURNALING

EXTRA JOURNALING

EXTRA JOURNALING

ENDNOTES

1. This model is built on an experiential education framework originally proposed by Laura Joplin and later modified and tested by Terry Linhart on youth ministry short-term mission trips. See Laura Joplin, "On Defining Experiential Education" in K. Warren, M. Sakofs, and J. S. Hunt Jr., eds., *The Theory of Experiential Education* (Dubuque, IA: Kendall/Hunt, 1995), 15–22; and Terrence D. Linhart, "Planting Seeds: The Curricular Hope of Short-Term Mission Experiences in Youth Ministry," *Christian Education Journal* 3 (2005): 256–72. For the purposes of this curriculum, some of the terminology in the model has been modified.

2. Adapted from Chap Clark and Kara E. Powell, *Deep Justice in a Broken World* (Grand Rapids: Zondervan, 2008), 11–12.

3. This prayer of review was adapted from pray-as-you-go.org, a website of Jesuit Media Initiatives.

4. Dom Hélder Câmara, *Dom Hélder Câmara: Essential Writings*, Francis McDonah, ed. (Maryknoll, NY: Orbis, 2009), 11.

5. Nicholas Wolterstorff, "The Contours of Justice: An Ancient Call for Shalom," in *God and the Victim: Theological Reflections on Evil, Victimization, Justice, and Forgiveness*, ed. Lisa Barnes Lampman and Michelle D. Shattuck (Grand Rapids: Eerdmans, 1999), 113.

6. Adapted from David A. Livermore's *Serving with Eyes Wide Open* (Grand Rapids: Baker, 2006).

7. Adapted from *YouthWorks! 2007 Devotional Journal*. Used with permission.

8. Adapted from Tim Dearborn, *Short-Term Missions Workbook: From Mission Tourist to Global Citizen* (Downers Grove, IL: InterVarsity, 2003), 94–96.

9. Ibid.

10. *The World Factbook*, last updated August 2014; see cia
.gov/library/publications/the-world-factbook/ and the
International Database for the US Census Bureau: census
.gov/population/international/data/idb/informationGateway
.php.

11. The descriptions of these disciplines are adapted from
Richard Foster's *Celebration of Discipline* (San Francisco:
HarperCollins, 1978).